Is My Dog in Heaven?

A Biblical Answer

Robert Hunt

Illustrations by Keil Alderson

VANTAGE PRESS
New York

Published by Vantage Press, Inc.
516 West 34th Street, New York, New York 10001

Manufactured in the United States of America
ISBN: 0-533-11469-1

Library of Congress Catalog Card No.: 95-90121

0 9 8 7 6 5 4 3 2 1

Contents

Preface

The material in this study began as a Sunday evening Bible study for my parishioners. I am indebted to participants in that study for their encouragement to put it in this present form. I am also grateful to Nancy I. Sanders for her editorial assistance and for her valuable suggestions and to Keil Alderson for his illustrations to accompany the text. It is now offered to those who appreciate all of heaven's treasures. Biblical quotations, unless otherwise noted, are from the Authorized Version.

Introduction

"Is my dog in heaven?"

That was my question as a teenager. That was when Brownie died. It has been my question since.

Brownie and I began life together as "puppies" and grew up companions. He walked me to school, faithfully waiting for me in the afternoons until school let out. At about five years of age, I decided to run away from home for an adventure; Brownie ran with me, and he also rode home with me in the patrol car. We rarely separated.

Brownie was playmate, friend, drier of childhood tears with a moist tongue, and personal guardian. I recall snuggling between his paws pouring out sobs of self-pity to what I knew was his sympathetic ear. Brownie was my buddy. When he died there seemed no question that we would have the same hope and the same reward at the end of our lives.

After Brownie died, my assumption was challenged. I heard: "Animals do not have souls," "They are just dumb beasts," "Heaven is for people," and variations on those themes. I could not accept such pronouncements uncritically. To me they didn't ring true for Brownie.

Animals had been a significant part of my growing up. My grandmother and a nearby cousin raised chickens, ducks, guineas, goats, cows, mules, and horses. I spent most of my childhood with these animal friends. Such an array of friends could not be lost forever.

I felt a strong bonding with animals and my memories of them remain fond and dear, memories of feelings shared and of personalities observed: Oscar the pig always ambling to his fence and calling me to come chat with him; Maude the mule keeping a vigilant eye for me. Each time I appeared, she sauntered over to visit.

The chickens and I played games together. A favorite of mine was my version of Rock-a-bye the Baby. Holding a chicken in the palms of both hands and gently rocking back and forth until the hen closed her eyes in sleep, I could place her head under her wing and cradle her like a baby. I discovered in this game that when you rock a chicken's body, the head remains stationary. Those chickens were so trusting of me that I could visit even the nesting hens and they would be unperturbed.

Those animals of my childhood I still remember by name and personality. They were special and they were friends. They bent a sympathetic ear and listened patiently and eagerly to my fantasies and troubles. I think of Bossie, my grandmother's old heifer, and how when listening to one of my sad childhood tales of woe, I saw a tear roll from her big, sympathetic eye. Brownie wasn't the only one whose supposed exclusion from eternity I questioned. These animal friends simply could not be lost forever.

Apparently I am not alone in this feeling. Elizabeth Marshall Thomas, author of *The Hidden Life of Dogs* (Boston/New York: Davison/Houghton Mifflin, 1993), reports that at signings for her book, individuals frequently ask her, "Do animals have souls?" Her reply, "If we have souls, then dogs have souls; and if we go to heaven so do they." And Thomas adds, "Because if dogs are not there it is not heaven." In Thomas's comment I recognize a kindred spirit.

When I first saw a figure of Francis of Assisi holding a bird resting in his hand and his glancing kindly toward it, I felt an affinity at once. Later, I discovered him depicted with many different animals, such as dogs, lambs, and deer. I felt a bond with this man from the thirteenth century.

When I read *The Little Flowers of Saint Francis*, a record of his life by members of his order, I confirmed the sense of kinship. His celebration of all God's creation and his belief that God created every animal to reflect an element of the Creator and to teach us about Himself found a witness of truth in my spirit.

In the experience of Francis, I felt support for my instinctive feeling about Brownie. I learned why Francis is always depicted with a bird. In *The Little Flowers*, there is a report of Francis on one of his journeys through the countryside. Upon viewing a field of thousands of birds of a variety of species, he felt compelled to preach to them.

The saint called on the birds to be grateful to God that they may fly so freely wheresoever they will, are clothed in coats of such beauty, have beautiful voices with which to sing, and are provided for without sowing or toiling for their food. The report is that the birds gathered around him, listened intently as he spoke, and burst into beautiful song when he had finished.

There are other reports of Francis and the birds. Once he rescued some doves from a boy taking them to be sold at market. He sent them on their way with instructions to be grateful to God for their rescue. On another occasion, he commanded the noisy swallows of Alviano to be quiet that he might speak to the crowd gathered in the square. They fell silent and listened intently to him as he preached.

The significant feature in these reports is that to Francis and to those who observed and reported these instances the creatures seemed aware of and responsive to a message about their Creator. To these observers it was not meaningless to preach to animals.

A report from the same time period explains how Anthony of Padua preached to the fish of Rimini. The report says that the fish gathered by thousands from the sea and the river's mouth at Rimini to listen carefully to Anthony's sermon, responding with joy. Again, the minimal significance of these instances is that to the participants and to those who recorded these events there was considered an appropriateness in preaching to the creatures. Here is evidence at least as far back as the thirteenth century of a tradition of the Gospel for the creatures. Is there a firm foundation for such a tradition?

With my obvious sympathies, through the years I came to be known among friends as "an animal lover." Acquaintances as well as strangers who have lost pets have asked me the question, "Is my pet in heaven?" I am not alone in wanting the question answered. But the answer must be more than a strong personal opinion, even if one shared by so saintly a figure as Francis of Assisi. To be of real value and comfort, the answer must have a firm assurance with a sound basis.

I believe that such an answer must be in biblical revelation. The Bible is where we find the certainty for the hope of heaven and eternity. We must, therefore, look in the Bible for the definitive word and our dependable answer.

Is My Dog in Heaven?

ONE

Creatures, Creation, and Re-Creation

The Bible opens with the creation story and the Creator God calling forth out of nothing light and darkness, the heavens, the earth, and the sea. Next, this setting of the world is populated with "every living creature which moveth within the waters," "every winged fowl of the air," and "every creeping thing and beast of the earth." Finally, God completes His creation with man (Gen. 1).

God calls this creation "very good." When it is complete, God rests and takes His pleasure. This is obviously creation as God desires it to be. A striking feature of this creation in Eden is the harmony that prevails between man and all nature, particularly between man and the creatures. Man is given the role of custodian of the creatures and is told to name each in turn.

The task as namer of the creatures holds a deep significance. In Hebrew consciousness, a name is the embodiment of the nature of the named. The giving of a name implies a special relationship to the subject. For instance, when Abram entered a covenant relationship with God, he is renamed Abraham (Gen. 17:5). When Jacob wrestles with an angel through the night and prevails, he is renamed Israel (Gen. 32:28). This tradition continues into the New Testament period as Simon becomes Peter and Saul is renamed Paul (Matt. 16:17–18; Acts 9:4).

1

Names among Hebrews are never casually or arbitrarily given. They signify something about the nature and/or task of the named and the relationship with the namer. "Thou shalt call his name Jesus for he shall save his people from their sins" (Matt. 1:21).

It is this Eden of man and creatures that man's rebellion interrupts and corrupts, making redemption a necessity. If sin had not intervened, Eden would appear today as God originally ordained it: man in harmony with the creatures and with all the world around him. This is the paradise lost; paradise regained will be a return to God's original intention.

This is explicit as the biblical revelation draws to its close and John sees God's restoration of His creation as "a new heaven and a new earth" (Rev. 21:1). This presence of all creatures in God's ideal once more appears in "the coming down from God of the holy city, the new Jerusalem" (Rev. 21:2).

Their presence is seen as John receives a glimpse into heaven. In his first vision of God's throne, John sees "every creature which is in heaven and on the earth and under the earth and such as are in the sea, and all that are in them." John hears the creatures saying, "Blessing and honor and glory and power be unto him that sitteth upon the throne and unto the Lamb for ever and ever" (Rev. 5:13).

The word translated "creature" is the same one used to denote all living things that God made. John's vision is of all creatures in God's presence joining in the worship and praise of heaven.

In the final vision of God's redemption fulfilled, John writes: "And he that sat upon the throne said, Behold, I make all things new" (Rev. 21:5). This "all things" (pas) used here means "all things that exist, all things created" and is the same word that is translated in the Prologue to John's Gospel when speaking of the Word who was in the beginning, "*all things* were made by him and without him was not anything made that was made" (John 1:3). It is also the word used when Paul writes that in Christ "*all things* are become new" (2 Cor. 5:17).

The presence of all creatures in John's vision of heaven, including their participation in heaven's worship and the celebration of the glory of God, is the culmination of a theme consistent throughout the biblical revelation.

In the eighth century before Christ, the prophet Isaiah pictured the coming day of the Lord's fulfillment of His redemptive work:

> The wolf also shall dwell with the Lamb, and the leopard shall lie down with the kid; and the calf and the young lion and the fatling together; and a little child shall lead them. And the cow and the bear shall feed; their young ones shall lie down together: and the lion shall eat straw like the ox. And the suckling child shall play on the hole of the asp, and the weaned child shall put his hand on the cockatrice's den. They shall not hurt nor destroy in all my holy mountain: for the earth shall be full of the knowledge of the Lord, as the waters cover the sea.
>
> (Isaiah 11: 6–9)

Quite clearly, Isaiah's picture of the Day of the Lord describes all creation in harmony, as it first originated in Eden. The picture definitely includes every creature.

A century later the prophet heralding the end of the Babylonian captivity likewise pictures the coming day of the Lord's redemption:

> The wolf and the lamb shall feed together, and the lion shall eat straw like the bullock: and dust shall be the

3

serpent's meat. They shall not hurt nor destroy in all my holy mountain, saith the Lord.

(Isaiah 65:25)

A striking feature explicit in this passage and in the one previously noted is the new state of harmony among the creatures themselves. Specific phrases combine to declare a reign of peace among the creatures and an end to their predatory existence. "The wolf shall dwell with the lamb." "The leopard shall lie down with the kid." "The cow and the bear shall feed." "Their young ones shall lie together." "The lion shall eat straw like the ox." "They shall not hurt nor destroy." Peace at last. This is a world in which survival and self-preservation are no longer necessities.

The contrast between the present state of nature and that of the peaceable kingdom in Isaiah is a commentary on the extent of the corruption of creation as a result of the fall of man. It produced chaos in the natural order and enmity among the creatures.

The hymn book of Israel continues the tradition of the inclusion of all creatures and creation in the celebration of God. "The earth is the Lord's and the fulness thereof, the world and they that dwell therein" (Ps. 24:1). Thus, when singing God's praise, all creation is called to join in the chorus:

Sing to the Lord, *all* the earth!
All the earth shall worship thee and sing unto thee.

(Psalms 66:1,4)

Let the heaven and earth praise him, the seas, and *everything that moveth therein*.

(Psalms 69:34)

4

Let the heavens rejoice, and let the earth be glad:
let the sea roar *and the fulness thereof.*
Let the field be joyful, and *all that is therein*: then
shall all the trees of the wood rejoice before the
Lord.

(Psalms 96:11–13)

The Lord reigneth; let the earth rejoice.
The heavens declare his righteousness.

(Psalms 97:1,6)

Make a joyful noise unto the Lord, *all* the earth:
make a loud noise, and rejoice, and sing praise.
Let the sea roar, *and the fulness thereof*; the world,
and *they that dwell therein.* Let the floods clap
their hands: let the hills be joyful together
before the Lord.

(Psalms 98:4,7–9)

Praise ye the Lord. Praise ye the Lord from the
heavens: praise him in the heights.
Praise ye him, all his angels: praise ye him, all
his hosts.
Praise ye him, sun and moon: praise ye him, all ye
stars of light.
Praise him, ye heavens of heavens, and ye waters that
be above the heavens.
Let them praise the name of the Lord; for he commanded
and they were created.
*He hath also stablished them for ever and ever:
he hath made a decree which shall not pass.*
Praise the Lord from the earth, ye dragons, and all
deeps:
Fire, and hail: snow, and vapour; stormy wind

fulfilling his word:

Mountains, and all hills; fruitful trees, and all
cedars:

*Beasts, and all cattle; creeping things, and flying
fowl:*

Kings of the earth, and all people; princes and all
judges of the earth:

Both young men, and maidens; old men, and children:

Let them praise the name of the Lord: for his name
alone is excellent; his glory is above the earth and
heaven.

He also exalteth the horn of his people, the praise of
all his saints; even of the children of Israel, a
people near unto him. Praise ye the Lord.

(Psalm 148)

(*emphasis added*)

And this is the verse with which the Book of Psalms
ends: "Let *everything that hath breath* praise the Lord.
Praise ye the Lord" (Ps. 150:6).

In Israel's book of worship, there is a clear sense of
all creatures and all creation caught up in the celebration
and praise of God, especially the celebration of God the
Redeemer. The terms "all the earth" and "all that dwell
therein" are all-inclusive. The praise of all the creatures
is loudly heard in the coming Day of the Lord.

The songs of Isaiah celebrate the redemptive work
of God's suffering servant and the coming Messiah. These
include: "The mountains and the hills shall break forth
before you into singing, and all the trees of the field shall
clap their hands. Instead of the thorn shall come up the
fig tree, and instead of the brier shall come up the myrtle
tree: and it shall be to the Lord for a name, for an

everlasting sign that shall not be cut off" (Isa. 55:12–13). Eden is restored!

This peaceable kingdom of God's restored creation has a foretaste in *The Little Flowers of Saint Francis.* In the village of Gubbio, villagers feel frightened of a wolf who terrorizes their town. Francis visits the village. He encounters the wolf who surprisingly comes to him with humbleness and submissiveness. Francis brings the townspeople and the wolf together, negotiating a pact between them. The wolf no longer ravishes the village nor their herds but visits their homes each morning to be fed as a household pet. The villagers celebrate this peace with the wolf as a goodness of the Lord.

In the Sermon on the Mount, Jesus uses an illustration that assumes an agreement among his hearers about God's providential care of the creatures: "Behold the fowls of the air; they sow not, neither do they reap, nor gather into barns; yet your heavenly Father feedeth them" (Matt. 6:26). And later more pointedly, he says, "Are not two sparrows sold for a farthing? and one of them shall not fall on the ground without your Father" (Matt. 10:29). Jesus assumes that the Heavenly Father provides for the creatures.

Long ago the Psalmist had declared plainly "the Lord preserveth both man and beast" (Ps. 36:6). In the biblical revelation, God's creatures are envisioned in God's world at creation as well as in that world's re-creation. They are participating in God's worship, praise, and the celebration of His redemptive glory.

Eden, Isaiah's Day of the Lord, Israel's songs of praise and celebration, John's vision of heaven—the creatures are included in all of these. God's redemption is a restoration of Eden, the renewal of His original "good" creation. This is how God made it and how God will reinstate His ultimate fulfillment of creation. The creatures are in Eden at creation; they are restored to Eden at the re-creation.

TWO

Creatures and the Covenant

In the Old Testament, there are two mighty acts of God that serve as prototypes for God's work of redemption: the Great Flood of Noah's time and the Exodus of the Children of Israel from Egypt.

In addition we have the covenant into which God enters with Israel at Sinai as the basis for God's being their god and their being His people. This covenant serves as prologue to the New Covenant in Jesus Christ. These are the Bible's revelations of God's redemption and promise of heaven. The creatures clearly are included in all these promises for the future.

The Great Flood

One does not recall God's covenant with Noah without picturing the parade of animals entering the Ark. God gives Noah instructions for the building of the ark as means of rescue from God's impending judgment on sinful man. God commands Noah to take his family aboard the Ark to be saved from the Flood. "And of every living thing of all flesh, two of every sort shalt thou bring into the ark, to keep them alive with thee; they shall be male and female. Of fowls after their kind, and of cattle

10

after their kind, of every creeping thing of the earth after his kind, two of every sort shall come unto thee, to keep them alive" (Gen. 6:19–20).

As the Ark floats upon the Flood, it is noted, "And God remembered Noah and every living thing and all the cattle that was with him in the ark" (Gen. 8:1). When the Ark lands, "Every beast, every creeping thing, and every fowl, and whatsoever creepeth upon the earth, after their kinds, went forth out of the ark" (Gen. 8:19).

The Flood is God's judgment. The Ark stands as God's provision of rescue from that judgment (redemption). The passengers aboard the Ark are the redeemed. As Noah's family represent mankind, so every thing is likewise represented aboard the Ark.

The stated intention is more explicit than the symbolism of the Ark and its passengers. After the disembarkation from the Ark, God declares:

And I, behold, I establish my covenant with you, and with your seed after you; And with every living creature that is with you, of the fowl, of the cattle, and of every beast of the earth with you; from all that go out of the ark, to every beast of the earth. And I will establish my covenant with you, neither shall all flesh be cut off any more by the waters of a flood; neither shall there be any more a flood to destroy the earth.

(Genesis 9:9–11)

As God sets the rainbow in the sky as the symbol of this covenant, He reiterates with whom this covenant is established. "And God said, This is the token of the covenant which I make between me and you and every living creature that is with you *for a perpetual generation*" (Gen. 9:12—*emphasis added*).

11

It is unmistakable that "every living creature" is included in the redemption of Noah's Flood. There is also explicit assurance that the promise made in the covenant after the Flood stands perpetually.

The Exodus

In the deliverance from Egyptian bondage into the land of promise, we find the symbolic inclusion of God's creatures. When Pharaoh inquires for whom Moses requests permission to depart, "And Moses said, We will go with our young and with our old, with our sons and with our daughters, with our flocks and with our herds will we go" (Exod. 10:9). Moses later adds, "Our cattle also shall go with us; there shall not a hoof be left behind" (Exod. 10:26).

In the warning of each plague by which Moses sought Pharaoh's permission for departure, it is specifically noted where animals are concerned that in a plague that might threaten Israel's cattle and flocks, they are to be spared from its consequences (Exod. 9:4,19; 11:7).

Most significant is the final plague of the angel of death passing over the land, sparing the firstborn of all those who have the blood of the lamb sprinkled upon the doorways of their houses. The cattle and flocks of Israel are also spared by the blood of the lamb in this night of Passover.

Afterward the Lord declared, "Sanctify unto me all the first-born, whatsoever openeth the womb among the children of Israel, both of man and of beast: it is mine" (Exod. 13:2).

In the Exodus from Egypt, the animals of Israel are

included in the request to be set free, they are spared judgment by the blood of the Lamb, and they cross the Red Sea from the land of bondage to the land of promise. They are partakers of every element of the redemptive symbolism. Afterward, God specifically includes them with those who are to be "sanctified" or set aside for Him.

The Sinai Covenant

The Law given to Moses on Mount Sinai is addressed to the obedience of man. After all, the need of redemption has been predicated by the disobedience of man. These commandments reveal how God wishes it to be in His world. The relationship God desires between Himself and man and between men is quite clearly defined.

At a significant point in the commandments, animals are included. It is in the fourth commandment requiring that the Sabbath day be kept holy. There is an enumeration of those whom this commandment enjoins. Those specified are "thou, thy son, thy daughter, thy manservant, thy maidservant, *thy cattle*, and the stranger within thy gates" (Exod. 20:10—*emphasis added*).

The injunction calls for the cattle to keep that day holy, a day described as "the sabbath of the Lord thy God" (Exod. 20:10), a day which the Lord blessed and hallowed (Exod. 20:11). In other words, animals are to share in the Lord's Sabbath.

The significance of this invitation is seen when one considers the meaning of the Sabbath. This is one of the few commandments for which a rationale is given: "For in six days the Lord made heaven and earth, the sea and all that in them is, and rested the seventh day" (Exod.

13

20:11). Thus Sabbath rest becomes participation in and commemoration of that rest of the Lord after completion of the work of creation. This rest does not convey a sense of recovery from the weariness of creative labors. God is and has ever been the God Who "neither sleeps nor slumbers" (Ps. 121:4). Rather His rest is satisfaction—shalom, peace—at the completion of something very good. The status of seventh day as the Sabbath of the Lord forms a basis for the number seven coming to represent in Hebrew consciousness the idea of fullness and completion.

The seventh day, the Sabbath, is the day God celebrates His pleasure at the completion of His "good Creation." Satisfaction and joy in the creation is behind God's blessing and sanctifying of this day (Gen. 2:3). In the Sinai covenant, God invites the creation to celebrate the Sabbath as a prototype and foreshadowing of the restoration of God's creation. It is a participation in the expectation of redemption. This is the commandment in which God specifies the cattle to be included.

As a symbol in time, God calls for one day in each seven to mark the promise and expectation of redemption. Likewise, one year in each seven years is specified as a Sabbath year and is to include "thy cattle" and "the beasts that are in thy land" (Lev. 25:7). That portion of the Sinai covenant, the Sabbath observance, which is commemoration of God's completion and fulfilling of His creation calls for inclusion of the creatures.

Through Hosea, the prophet of the eighth century before Christ, God reiterates His inclusion of the creatures in His covenant: "And in that day will I make a covenant for them with the beasts of the field and with the fowls of heaven and with the creeping things of the ground: and I will break the bow and the sword and the

14

battle out of the earth, and will make them to lie down safely" (Hos. 2:18).

It is very clear that the creatures are represented in the redemption of the Ark in the Great Flood and in the Exodus from Egyptian bondage—those mighty acts of God foreshadowing the redemption of the world. They are beneficiaries of the covenants made with Noah and made with Moses and the children of Israel at Sinai. This is the background of God's New Covenant in Jesus Christ.

The New Covenant in Christ.

The more familiar proclamations of the good news in Jesus Christ are:

> For God so loved the world that he gave his only begotten Son that whosoever believeth in him should not perish but have eternal life. For God sent not his Son into the world to condemn the world; but that the world through him might be saved.
>
> (John 3:16–17)

> God was in Christ reconciling the world unto himself.
>
> (2 Corinthians 3:19)

And there is that proclamation with which the ministry of Jesus begins: "The next day John seeth Jesus coming unto him and saith, Behold the Lamb of God which taketh away the sin of the world" (John 1:29).

There is one recurring word designating the object of God's redemptive work in Christ. "God so loved the *world*," "not to condemn the *world*," "that the *world*

15

through him might be saved," "reconciling the *world* unto himself," "taketh away the sin of the *world.*" Christ's work of redemption is for "the world."

Wherever the word translated "world" is used in the New Testament, it is understood to be inclusive of all God's creation. There can be no doubt for whom the good news in Christ is intended. It is intended for the world, which definitely includes the creatures.

When describing the effect of Christ's coming, the Apostle Paul writes: "Therefore if any man be in Christ, he is a new creature: old things are passed away; behold, *all things are become new*" (2 Cor. 5:17).

A more explicit passage in which Paul is particularly addressing the subject of the redemption of creation and the creatures is:

> For the earnest expectation of the creature waiteth for the manifestations of the sons of God. For the creature was made subject to vanity, not willingly, but by reason of him who hath subjected the same in hope, because *the creature itself also shall be delivered from the bondage of corruption into the glorious liberty of the children of God.* For we know that *the whole creation groaneth and travaileth in pain together until now.* And not only they, but ourselves also, which have the first-fruits of the Spirit, even we ourselves groan within ourselves, *waiting for the adoption, to wit, the redemption of our body*
> (Romans 8:19–23—*emphasis added*)

This is a traditional translation of this passage. However, a modern paraphrase of it remains true to its implication but is more explicit:

> For all creation is waiting patiently and hopefully for that future day when God will resurrect his children. For on

16

that day thorns and thistles, sin, death, and decay—the things that overcame the world against its will at God's command—will all disappear, and the world around us will share in the glorious freedom from sin which God's children enjoy.

For we know that even the things of nature, like animals and plants, suffer in sickness and death as they await this great event. And even we Christians, although we have the Holy Spirit within us as a foretaste of future glory, also groan to be released from pain and suffering. We, too, wait anxiously for that day when God will give us our full rights as his children, including the new bodies he has promised us—bodies that will never be sick again and will never die.

(The Living Bible)

Paul also writes to the church at Colosse, speaking of God the Father:

Who hath delivered us from the power of darkness, and hath translated us into the kingdom of his dear Son: in whom we have redemption through his blood, even the forgiveness of sins: who is the image of the invisible God, *the first born of every creature:* for by him were all things created that are in heaven and that are in earth, visible and invisible, whether they be thrones or dominions or principalities or powers: *all things* were created *by* him and *for* him . . . by him *all things* consist. . . . that in *all things* he might have the preeminence. For it pleased the Father that in him should *all fulness* dwell. And having made peace through the blood of his cross, by him *to reconcile all things unto himself,* by him, I say, whether they be things in earth or things in heaven.

(Colossians 1:15–20—emphasis added)

How much more emphatic could the New Testament

be that the creatures are in Christ's redemption? They share in the rescue from the Flood of Noah's time and in the release from Egyptian bondage in Moses' day, the two mighty acts of God's redemption. They are included in the perpetual promise of God's covenant with Noah and in the Sabbath rest of the Sinai covenant. And they are among the all things Christ has reconciled to himself.

THREE

Animals as Sacrifice and Image

When one thinks of animals in the Scriptures, there comes to mind most readily their inclusion aboard Noah's Ark and then their place in Israel's sacrificial system. The two pictures seem at odds.

Israel was instructed to bring to the priests offerings of their cattle, herds, and flocks (Lev. 1:2). The focal point in the court of the tabernacle, and later the temple, to which the congregation of Israel came for their feasts and celebration of God was the altar upon which these sacrifices were made.

A peace offering was to be from the herd (Lev. 3:1); a sin offering, a young bullock (Lev. 4:3); a trespass offering, a lamb or kid of the goats (Lev. 5:6). The Book of Leviticus details the offerings acceptable, their preparation for and method of sacrifice, as well as the disposition of the sacrificial remains.

The most prominent sacrifice in Israel's worship was the Passover Lamb, which had enabled the Exodus from Egypt. The blood of that lamb rescued God's people from death and permitted their deliverance from captivity to the land of promise. That lamb would ever afterward be remembered and commemorated in the high festival of the Jewish year. This symbol of the Passover Lamb remains central in Jewish worship to this day.

As the Hebrew experience of God continued and their

understanding of God became fuller, awareness grew in Israel's consciousness that animal sacrifice was not the will of God and indeed not what He required of His people. As early as the reign of Israel's first king, the prophet Samuel declared: "And Samuel said, Hath the Lord as great delight in burnt offerings and sacrifices as in obeying the voice of the Lord? Behold, to obey is better than sacrifice and to harken than the fat of rams" (1 Sam. 15:22).

This consciousness continued to grow with God's people:

Sacrifice and offering thou didst not desire; mine ears hast thou opened: burnt offering and sin offering hast thou not required.

(Psalms 40:6)

For thou desirest not sacrifice; else would I give it: thou delightest not in burnt offerings. The sacrifices of God are a broken spirit: a broken and a contrite heart, O God, thou wilt not despise.

(Psalms 51:16–17)

There comes an increasing awareness that what God requires of man is not something to be brought and left with Him, but rather that God's desire is that man offer something of himself. "To do justice and judgment is more acceptable to the Lord than sacrifice" (Prov. 21:3).

This awareness becomes a conviction of the will of God in the prophets of the eighth and seventh century before Christ.

I have desired mercy and not sacrifice; and the knowledge of God more than burnt offerings.

(Hosea 6:6)

21

I hate, I despise your feast days, and I will not smell in your solemn assemblies. Though you offer me burnt offerings and your meat offerings, I will not accept them: neither will I regard the peace offerings of your fat beasts. Take thou away from me the noise of thy songs; for I will not hear the melody of thy viols. But let judgment run down as waters and righteousness as a mighty stream.

(Amos 5:21–24)

The conviction takes root as Jeremiah hears God declare: "your burnt offerings are not acceptable nor your sacrifices sweet unto me" (Jer. 6:20). The prophet Micah concludes,

Wherewith shall I come before the Lord and bow myself before the high God? shall I come before him with burnt offerings, with calves of a year old? Will the Lord be pleased with thousands of rams or with ten thousands of rivers of oil? shall I give my first-born for my transgression, the fruit of my body for the sin of my soul? He hath showed thee, O man, what is good; and what doth the Lord require of thee but to do justly, and to love mercy, and to walk humbly with thy God?

(Micah 6:6–8)

As regards animal sacrifice, the faith of Israel progressively draws closer to that position which is found in the new covenant in Jesus Christ:

I beseech you, therefore, brethren, that you present your bodies a living sacrifice.

(Romans 12:1)

22

Let us offer the sacrifice of praise to God continually, that is, the fruit of our lips giving thanks to his name. But to do good and to communicate forget not: for with such sacrifices God is well pleased.

(Hebrews 13:15–16)

With the fuller understanding of God's will, it becomes increasingly clear that the offering of animal sacrifices is not pleasing nor acceptable to God.

This might seem to the modern mind a higher appreciation of the value of animals. However, that is not necessarily so. We have a different sensitivity to cruelty and a sense of response to God fashioned by the moral climate created by the teachings of Jesus.

Were we able to share the same frame of reference and values of the ancient mind without the fullness of light revealed in Jesus Christ, we might better appreciate the meaning of animal sacrifice in that time and, therefore, the regard of the animals offered.

Our modern definition of sacrifice has undergone subtle adjustment across time. It now involves connotations of "giving something up, destroying or foregoing." The accent is on denying and surrender. The implications of the word are essentially negative.

We are now too schooled in the theology of grace and unmerited salvation to fathom appreciably the frame of mind if one were without it. If that were our condition and then we knew that there should be something we might offer by which such unattainable benefit might be ours, would we not offer it with eagerness and joy? This was the religious condition of the ancient Hebrew. His sacrifice gave him the same thrill that is ours in the acceptance of the reconciliation to God through Jesus Christ.

23

The ancient sacrifice was not a cast-off, disposable value. On the contrary, the sacrificial instructions include every insistence to assure its value. The repeated description of the offering is that it must be "without blemish" (Exod. 12:5; Lev. 5:15). It must be the best.

Far more significant is the understanding of the value that the sacrificed animals represented to the Lord. The striking feature of the sacrificial system is that the animals were "a sacrifice for man's sin," and able to make "atonement for sin." By them, sin was forgiven (Lev. 5:14–18). On Israel's Day of Atonement, a scapegoat upon whom the priest laid hands bore all the people's iniquities and "all their transgressions in all their sins" (Lev. 16:21).

The only other biblical revelation acceptable to God as an atonement for man's sin and by whom He would forgive sin is His Son Jesus Christ (John 3:16–17). In the created order, none other than animals were given such an exalted position of representation. The animal sacrifices are described as "pleasing to the Lord" (Lev. 8:21) and declared to be "most holy" (Lev. 6:17; 7:1,6). Animals have an exalted position in the sacrificial system. They are prototypes of the Christ and are, in fact, the symbols and instruments of God's redemption.

The pleasing and acceptable regard in which the ancients believed God held animals continues in the consciousness of Israel beyond the sacrificial system into the New Testament. The Psalmist believed God preserved the beasts. They were continually included in the celebration songs of God's glory and goodness through the time when Jesus assured that no sparrow falls without God's awareness.

The more telling evidence of this divine regard is the appropriateness with which animals are seen as images

24

of God. We already noted that animals in the sacrificial system were prototypes of Christ's work of atonement. One of the dominant symbols by which Christ is identified is as the Lamb of God, the Christian Passover Lamb, releasing mankind from captivity to freedom by the offering up of Himself.

John the Baptist introduces Jesus at the beginning of His ministry: "Behold the Lamb of God who takes away the sin of the world" (John 1:29). Note once more "the world" as the object of the redemptive work.

Jesus is also referred to as "the Lion of Judah" (Rev. 5:5). In more subtle ways, an affinity for animals must be inferred from such associations as Jesus' identification of Himself as the Good Shepherd (John 10:14), a role inescapably associated with the care of sheep.

There is no avoiding the animal connection with the incarnation of the Redeemer God. The first public proclamation of the coming of the Messiah is to shepherds "keeping watch over their flocks" (Luke 2:8) and Christ is born in a stable and cradled in a manger (Luke 2:7). The Bread of Life first rests in the abode and feeding place of animals.

The third person of the Trinity, the Holy Spirit, is symbolized as a descending dove (Mark 1:10 and parallel passages). The dove is the only concrete symbol in the New Testament of the Holy Spirit.

Even God the Father, the Jehovah of the Old Testament, for whom it is strictly forbidden that there should be any image or "likeness of anything that is in heaven above or that is in the earth beneath or that is in the water under the earth" (Exod. 20:4) is described by similies to animals. He is described "like as a lion and a young lion roaring" (Isa. 31:4–5) and as a leopard and "a bear that is bereaved of her whelps" (Hos. 13:7–8).

God's special regard for animals is unmistakable when they are described as "pleasing to the Lord" and "holy to the Lord." They must have extraordinary value to God that He should find them acceptable to merit being the means of His forgiveness of man. It would be God's only Son who would greater fulfill that role. Also there must be an affinity shown for them in emphasizing their appropriateness as images to convey to us something of the divine nature and work.

Their place in the sacrificial system was quite the opposite of disregard for their value. Only the work of Christ and the repentance and obedience of man could be of greater redemptive value. From the beginning, animals have been continuously involved both as objects for and symbols of God's redemptive work.

FOUR

Do Animals Have Souls?

"Animals don't have souls."

I've heard this statement declared with finality, and I've wondered how it became so unquestionable a truth for the speaker. There is no biblical text to affirm it. Yet there are some who believe it and believe it proof that animals can't possibly partake of eternal life.

The dictum seems more proof of the degree of secularization of some theology. The immortality of the soul as a prerequisite to eternity is not a Christian concept, nor a Jewish one, but more a product of Greek philosophy or Eastern mysticism. It originates in Plato's teachings rather than in Scripture. The Christian basis of eternity rests on the resurrection of the body, not on the indestructibility of an aspect of our being which we call "the soul." The Christian creed from the beginning has been an affirmation of belief "in the resurrection of the body" (The Apostles' Creed, The Nicene Creed, etc.).

The distinction between man with soul and animals without may have been fostered by biblical translators' choice of words. The King James Authorized Version of the Scriptures of 1611 translates the Hebrew word *nephest* in Genesis 2:7 as "living soul": "And the Lord God formed man of the dust of the ground, and breathed into his nostrils the breath of life; and man became a *living soul*." Yet when referring to creatures the same

27

word is translated differently: "And God said, Let the earth bring forth *the living creature* after his kind, cattle, and creeping thing and beast of the earth after his kind: and it was so" (Gen. 1:24—*emphasis added*).

It would have been as linguistically valid to translate the former "and man became *a living creature*" and the latter, "Let the earth bring forth *the living soul* after his kind." The difference is in the choice of the translator according to his reading of the context. In the Hebrew text, the words are identical.

This word *nephest* means in Hebrew "soul, life, person, living being, blood, breath, living creature" and is translated in English versions according to the choice of the translator. It is used of man as in Genesis 2:7 and Genesis 2:19. It is likewise used in reference to animals as in Genesis 1:20,24,30 and Genesis 9:12,15,16. The English translation sometimes make a distinction that is not necessarily made in the original text.

Translators' choices together with Greek influence (the immortality of the soul) on Western thought may have drastically contributed to the distinction. A sharp distinction is not clearly defined in the biblical texts.

However, there is an aspect of being that is other than the physical designated in Scripture by "soul." This is apparent in texts such as, "And now, Israel, what does the Lord thy God require of thee but to fear the Lord thy God, to walk in all his ways and to love him and to serve him with all thy heart and with all thy soul" (Deut. 10:12).

The same distinction is likewise found in the New Testament: "And thou shalt love the Lord thy God with all thy heart and with all thy soul and with all thy mind and with all thy strength: this is the first commandment" (Mark 12:30).

Through the centuries it has been the burden of

theology to define what is the soul. There has been uniform agreement that this soul is the nonphysical quality of existence and the greater majority of theologians have concluded that the soul of man is not a separate entity from the spirit of man—in other words, man is not trichotomic.

> That man consists of soul and body, ought not to be controverted. By "soul" I understand an immortal, yet created essence, which is the nobler part of him. Sometimes it is called a "spirit"; for though when these names are connected, they have a different signification, yet when "spirit" is used separately, it means the same as "soul."
>
> (John Calvin, *Institutes*, Book I, Chapter XV)

The consensus of biblical scholarship and theology has found the soul discernible through its faculties or attributes, and most have found these best defined in the capacity for knowing and willing.

> The human soul has two faculties which relate to our present design, the understanding and the will. Now, let it be the office of the understanding to discriminate between objects, as they shall respectively appear deserving of approbation or disapprobation; but of the will, to choose and follow what the understanding shall have pronounced to be good; to abhor and avoid what it shall have condemned.
>
> (John Calvin, ibid.)

As Calvin also points out in the work cited, these faculties of the soul are inclusive of understanding, reason, imagination, will, and the irascible and concupiscible faculties (i.e., strong emotions). In other words, the presence of the soul is confirmed by the presence of reason, emotion, and decision.

I have experienced all these faculties in animals I have known. And I have encountered multi-evidence of them in animals about whom I have read and heard.

My Siberian husky, Barnabas, repeatedly demonstrates his ability to reason. He resents being confined in a fenced yard. He has nowhere to go nor does he wish to run away; whenever he "escapes" the fenced area, he immediately comes to the house entrance to scratch on the door for readmittance to the house. It is clear he is making a point: he is not going to be fenced in.

We live in a city with leash laws and busy thoroughfares. To me, our fencing is essential; to Barnabas, it is an effrontery and an infringement. Barnabas and I continuously face off in a battle of wits. From the first, he sought and found ways to circumvent the fence. He has found every weakness and frailty in its structure. He is an expert climber and we have gone from a six-foot to an eight-foot fence.

After months of this war of the fence, it seemed I had won. For nearly a week, I had relished my victory when I heard a scratch on the front door. I opened it and Barnabas paraded triumphantly into the house. I vainly searched the fence for its weakness. Meanwhile, Barnabas emphasized his mastery with that scratch on the front door.

Nearly certain he had outwitted me, one day I stood looking out my window. I noticed Barnabas in the corner of the yard behaving very curiously. I watched unseen. After a careful survey of the situation, he took off from the corner in a hurried dash toward the house. A few feet away, he leaped into the air, landed against the house, pushed off from it, did a sideways flip in mid-air, and sailed over the fence where it joined the house. I was amazed. Such an acrobatic feat could not have been accomplished without careful reasoning and planning. There had been no model to imitate.

I regularly take my dogs to our place in the country, a 125-mile journey that usually lasts hours. Barnabas knows the route well. He also associates the clicking of the turn indicator with our turns. When we approach a usual turn, he will look at the indicator until I put it on. Whenever I turn it on at an expected place, he immediately looks left and right to see the corner where we could be turning.

Another of my huskies, Mary Agnes, has also learned that route. Her particular affinity is for cows. She knows on our journey the pastures where they usually are. Before they come into view, she is ready at the window. If I should see a herd at some unaccustomed place and she is not on alert, I merely say, "Cows." She jumps to her post.

On these journeys all my dogs know when we are within the last few miles of our destination. The excitement and anticipation build as we approach. They also know if I detour or make unusual side trips. Their curiosity and inquiry are evident. They look at me and they look in the direction of our travel with clear expressions of puzzlement.

Sarah, the mother of my husky litter, has always been especially fond of our place in the country and had a special affection for our cousin, Benji, who lived there. She unmistakenly preferred him to me. When we were there on visits and she perceived that the time for departing was near, she would slip off and hide in the woods, not responding to my calls, in hopes that I would leave without her. She could remain with her Benji. My dogs plan and execute plots as well as retain and appropriately recall information.

Every dog owner has observed the uncanny perception of canines. My dogs know when we are going to the country. It is unrelated to how I am dressed or what preparations I make before the trip. I have deliberately guarded against giving any behavioral or visual clues and still they know. I can dress, follow the same routine, and leave without notice, but if I do the same and am going to the country, all the dogs gather eagerly at the door.

Dogs are more masterful than most human friends at judging one's mood. They respond appropriately to your joy and your sorrow. If you are happy, they are there to play and frolic. If you're tired, they are guarded but stay close to let you know they are near. If you are grieved, they are sympathetic, often nestling close to you or laying a head in your lap. My dogs read me well and respond with appropriate understanding.

My experience of canine understanding and sensitivity convinces me of their emotional life. They grieve as humans do. If I'm absent for a short while, my dogs' appetites begin to fade and other signs of depression emerge. They grieve not only for themselves and their human companions, but they grieve for one another. When Ranger, a poodle of eighteen years, had to be put to rest, Caesar, his companion of many years, mourned his absence for months. Caesar showed little interest in food, aloofness, and a lack of his typical zest.

Ranger's death gave me a deeper insight into the emotional perception of dogs. At the time I had two poodles, Ranger and Caesar, and Lu, a Belgian shepherd. Their favorite treat was canned corned beef. Whenever a can was opened, there was excited jockeying for the treat. On the morning Ranger was to be put to sleep, I opened a can of corned beef as a farewell treat. As Ranger lay eating his treat, Caesar and Lu stood across the room watching sadly, never wanting or expecting a morsel. They knew this was Ranger's and Ranger's alone, his parting token.

My experience has convinced me that they have the capacity to reason, to understand, to sympathize—in fact, to share the whole range of human emotions. The human capacity for these faculties may be more sophisticated, even more profound. However, in the perception of the thoughts and feelings of others and in devotion and faithfulness, the canine capacity often seems superior.

Two leading national news magazines within months of each other featured cover stories on the new scientific regard for the capacity of animals. *Time* (March 22, 1993) carried on its cover the question "Can Animals Think?" The answer included was: "Yes, and maybe even lie and play politics.New studies show how clever they can be."

In the accompanying article, there was a review of studies with a parrot who possesses a primitive ability to form plans, manipulate symbols, plot mischief, and express sentiment; a pygmy chimpanzee with a grammatical comprehension at the level of a 2½-year-old; dolphins and sea lions who master sign language and communicate with human trainers. Sharon Begley's and Joshua Cooper Ramo's article in *Newsweek* titled "Not Just Another Pretty Face"* carried a boldface heading: "They

*The following extracts are from NEWSWEEK, November 1, 1993, © 1993, Newsweek, Inc. All rights reserved. Reprinted by permission.

plan. They deceive. They solve problems in ways that demand more than basic instinct."

In the accompanying article (pages 63–67), the concern goes beyond intelligence:

> Researchers are trying to get past dolphins that respond to hand gestures from a trainer or the sea otter that masters transitive thought (if A is bigger than B, and B is bigger than C, then A . . .). Instead of asking whether animals can count and learn concepts like categories, ethologists are probing a question more profound and disturbing in its ethics implications: do animals think about thinking? Do they monitor their thoughts rather than just process information? Do they have an inner life, engage in introspection, rather than follow preset learned or genetic rules of behavior like an automation? Do they, in short, possess that sublime thing called consciousness?

In their review of current scientific studies with animals, they found: "Animals display forethought and make plans, they show insight into the minds of their kin and kind, and they adapt their behavior to deceive the minds of others. They understand situations in a way that suggests they hold a mental representation of the world, of what was and of what could be, not merely of what is."

There is no question that animals have a mental image of what they want, and they obviously are able to review options.

The conclusion to the *Newsweek* article:

> What makes these more than "amazing animal stories" is that they go beyond cute and clever. They point to a mind that does not act reflexively but weighs options, that recognizes belief in others, that can conceive possible

futures. Some animals are capable of more than rote learning and instinct; they think about what they know.

Current attention to the mystique of animals which discovers that they are more than dumb brutes encourages animal enthusiasts who have long felt something special about God's creatures. These discoveries may come as no news to those who have known animals well, but they should come welcomed by any who don't yet know so well all creatures great and small.

Mary Agnes, my husky, reasons quite well. Moreover, she has a skill for subtle deception and manipulation. There is her favored chair in our den, which sits beside a glass door into the garden; next to this door is a smaller door for the dogs. My cousin Ben was sitting in Agnes's chair. She came outside the glass door and scratched at the door to be admitted. Ben repeatedly pointed to the dog's door, saying, "Agnes, come in your door." She looked at the dog door and again scratched at the glass door. This exchange repeated itself over and over until Ben rose out of exasperation to open the door for her. As he rose, Agnes darted like a bullet through the dog door and into "her" chair. When Ben turned around, Agnes was comfortably resting with an air of total innocence in his former seat.

What makes one wonder about the superiority of Agnes's reasoning is that a few days later we were in the same situation, with the same exchange in progress between Ben and Agnes. It continued a little longer than before, but ultimately she wore Ben down. Frustrated, he cautiously rose to open the door for her, declaring, "You're not going to fool me again." But she did! Exactly as before!

Hannah, another husky, is a television fan. She

intently and regularly watches her favorite programs. Hannah knows when her programs are to come on, recognizes their theme music, and comes running from anywhere in the house to the television set on hearing the first bars of the theme. She knows programs that precede her favorites and when they are on will arrange herself before the set to await the start of "her" program.

Animals have the power to reason, to will, and to make and act on decisions with an awareness of consequences. They also experience a diverse range of emotions. The only qualification might be the extent of those qualities. Yet dimension cannot be a deciding factor concerning the faculties of the soul; otherwise there would arise problems with claiming a soul for undeveloped infants and mentally retarded persons.

A remaining question is whether animals have a moral sense, that is, whether they know right from wrong. I am convinced that they recognize wrong. Whenever Barnabas effected an escape from our fenced yard, his four sisters came excitedly to find me and lead me to the place he got out. There was no question they recognized he had done something "wrong" and were "telling on" him.

When one of my dogs makes a "mistake," all my dogs avoid the place as though any one of them might be blamed for doing something wrong. Yet only one of them can actually be guilty. If I correct one's behavior toward another dog, the corrected one knows he has done something wrong. Even before I make the correction, evidence already appears of the expectation of a reprimand.

In my experience animals are aware when they have done wrong. They show remorse and guilt. They even seek forgiveness.

One might argue that such awareness of right and

wrong is a product of training and conditioning by human masters. In response to this, I recall one illustration. Charlotte Edwards ("The Swan and the Goose," in *All God's Children* [1993]) reports the experience of a friend who lives near Oxford, Maryland. Sipping coffee one winter morning by a large window overlooking the Tred Avon River, the friend noticed a Canadian goose whose feet were frozen in the river's ice. She saw a line of swans flying across the sky. They landed in a circle about the goose.

The friend, Ms. Edwards writes, feared the goose was doomed to become their prey. To her surprise the swans began picking at the ice with their bills. They pecked for a long time until the goose was free and standing on the ice. The swans then hovered over him in the air, watching as the goose discovered his wings were covered in ice. "Then as if he had cried, 'I cannot fly,' four of the swans came down around him. Their powerful beaks scraped the goose's wings from bottom to top, scuttled under its wings and rode up its body, chipping off and melting the ice held in the feathers."** Their work of mercy done, the line of swans resumed their eastward journey. The goose flew after them, joining the end of their line.

A parishioner reported hearing a thud against her window. When she looked out to inquire, she saw a bird lying prone beneath the window. As she watched, the bird's mate flew down beside her, jumped on her breast, and began kneading her chest with his claws for what

**Reprinted with permission from *Guideposts* Magazine. Copyright ©1971 by Guideposts Associates, Inc. Carmel, New York 10512.

could only be an effort at artificial respiration. When he became aware that he was being watched, he grasped the bird's body and flew away with her into the woods.

I remember seeing at the curb of one of our busy city streets the corpse of a cardinal with her mate standing forlornly beside her, so stunned by his grief that he was unaware of the speeding traffic only a few feet away.

They grieve. They think. They feel.

Do animals have souls? The Hebrew word meaning either "living creature" or "living soul" is used of them in Scripture. We are increasingly aware of the extent to which they evidence the faculties of the soul that theology delineates. If there should be reason that the question cannot be answered unequivocally in the affirmative, there is certainly reason that it cannot emphatically be answered in the negative.

Quite unmistakably, as we have seen, animals are the objects of God's eternal love. According to the scriptural evidence, they do indeed have a place in heaven.

Now, the question of real import remains: how do we fulfill the ethical responsibility inherent in this fact?

FIVE

Man's Responsibility

Disorder and corruption were introduced into creation by the disobedience of man. His rebellion against God's command brought a curse to the created order: "Cursed is the ground for thy sake; in sorrow shalt thou eat of it all the days of thy life; thorns also and thistles shall it bring forth to thee" (Gen. 3:17–18).

The Apostle Paul writes "the creation was made subject to vanity, not willingly, but by reason of him who has subjected the same in hope" (Rom. 8:20). Man is responsible for the creatures' fallen state. The creatures are dependent upon man's reconciliation to God for their restoration. "For the earnest expectation of the creature waiteth for the manifestation of the sons of God" (Rom. 8:19).

The creatures waiting to be "delivered from the bondage of corruption into the glorious liberty of the children of God" are thus described: "For we know that the whole creation groaneth and travaileth in pain together until now" (Rom. 8:21–22). The term "travaileth" is one for the labor of childbirth. Creation is waiting to be born anew.

From the will and act of man has come the state that necessitates redemption: "since by man came death . . . as in Adam all die" (1 Cor. 15:21, 22). As man was the agent of creation's fall, so man is the agent of creation's redemption. Therefore, the promise of and the invitation

40

to God's redemption throughout the biblical revelation is addressed to the will and obedience of man. Man's response affects creation's fate.

Here is the measure of the significance of God's having made man "to dress and to keep" the Garden of His creation (Gen. 2:15). Man's assignment at creation was to have dominion over the creation and all the creatures (Gen. 1:28). That dominion clearly encompassed their fate in Eden and now as clearly encompasses their fate in heaven.

Noah and Moses were instructed to gather the creatures for inclusion in their experiences of God's mighty acts of redemption, the Ark and the Red Sea crossing. Likewise, in His commissioning of His disciples, Jesus gives similar instructions: "Go ye into all the world and preach the gospel to every creature" (Mark 16:15).

Preach the gospel to every creature. How might the responsibility be fulfilled? The thought of delivering sermons in field and forest to beast and fowl does not quite seem to be it, though Francis of Assisi did it. The "gospel" is the good news in Christ. The question is how might this good news be conveyed to creatures and creation.

Certainly, each one's personal response to this good news in Christ is the primary enabler for creation's restoration. As the Apostle Paul put it, "For the earnest expectation of the creature waiteth for the manifestation of the sons of God" (Rom. 8:19). Possibilities present themselves.

Jesus' final words to His disciples were: "Ye shall be witnesses unto me . . . to the uttermost parts of the earth" (Acts 1:8). His meaning is that the world shall see Him through these disciples. Earlier, He had said to them, "Ye are the light of the world" and "ye are the salt of the earth" (Matt. 5:13–14). The former meant that the

41

world would see the truth through them. The latter meant that they were a preservative and a seasoning for the world.

In terms of this responsibility to creation, the first obligation is to make known to creation and the creatures how God feels about His world, that He loves the world and desires to restore it to its created goodness. The world is the Lord's now and forever!

Again, how is this done in a practical and nonverbal proclamation? There is one truth repeatedly reinforced in the New Testament about Jesus' expectation in any response to Him. Jesus enjoins *actions* that speak.

> Not everyone that sayeth unto me, Lord, Lord . . . but he that doeth the will of my Father.
>
> > (Matthew 7:21)

> Therefore whosoever heareth these sayings of mine and doeth them, I will liken unto a wise man which buildeth his house upon a rock.
>
> > (Matthew 7:24)

> He that hath my commandments and keepeth them, he it is that loveth me.
>
> > (John 14:21)

There are actions by which we preach the gospel to every creature. There is the seriousness with which we undertake the God-given duty "to dress and to keep" the creation. This entails a responsibility to preserve and care for the whole creation and all God's creatures. This is the first responsibility God gave man, and it has been continuously reiterated since man's initial failure.

The assumption of personal responsibility is basic

for the protection of the environment, its clean-up and recovery from damage done. From the Bible's point of view, this has been the inherent responsibility of man from his creation.

Since the disruption of harmony among the creatures originated with man, man's obligation is to restore this God-given benefit to creation. God himself will fulfill it perfectly in His new creation. Until then, we are witnesses of God's love and purpose to a fallen world. Among the possibilities, action is necessitated for the prevention of cruelty to animals and their needless exploitation for human indulgence. If we know animals have sentience and emotion, we must examine how they are abused. Further, we must bear witness to God's concern for endangered species being lost to His creation. We cannot irresponsibly waste divine gifts.

More than defensive action on behalf of the creatures, there must be positive acts evidencing God's love of "the world." Animals do respond to loving kindness even as humans do. I have known animals who had been so mistreated and abused by humans that they grew distrustful and hostile toward people. These same animals, when exposed to care and loving kindness, became "new creatures."

Ranger, a poodle rescued from an animal shelter after much obvious abuse by former owners, found protective hiding places in the house. He moved from place to place by slinking along the walls, never coming out into the open spaces, not responding when called. He bit my hand the first time I reached toward him to pet him. After many months he became an animal that never wanted to leave your side. He would crawl into your lap for a nap.

Response to kind treatment is more obvious with

domesticated animals and more obscure for most wild animals. Yet the experience of trainers and animal ecologists with gorillas, monkeys, dolphins, sea otters, and other creatures from the wild indicates positive response to favorable human treatment. My personal experience has only been with animals more accustomed to some human proximity: birds, squirrels, deer. However, as a college student, I worked one summer on an alligator farm in Florida and made friends with a boa constrictor and particularly with an indigo snake who enjoyed afternoon naps with me. I never attempted to pet the alligators.

The potential for harmony among all creatures must exist if there is to be a day when the young child shall play upon the adder's hole or the lamb lie down with wolf. It has always seemed to me some special grace prevailed among the creatures aboard Noah's ark as they floated upon those ancient waters.

There is restorative work to be done in our treatment of creatures if we are to be faithful to God's commission. As we increasingly encroach upon their natural habitats, we must as increasingly assume responsibility for the availability of their food and shelter. It is God's will that they be inhabitants of the earth and God has given man responsibility as their caretakers. We must ultimately answer to God for this stewardship.

Each of us must determine the specifics of our response to this God-given responsibility for the creation. It is important for all of us, though, to realize that it is our God-given responsibility. We cannot neglect its obligation.

There are three kind ladies, living in the countryside with adequate acreage, who have found a mission in life to give a home to abused and stray animals. They give home to an array of dogs, cats, horses, goats, occasional birds, opossums and a raccoon. They have had nearly fifty dogs at one time among their residents. It's a pleasure to visit their enclave and be greeted by a sea of wagging tails and happy faces accompanied by a chorus of excited barking.

Canine skill for greeting and welcoming has long been a noticeable feature. My dogs, after even short separations of less than an hour, greet my return with the joy of a father receiving a returning prodigal. Each dog has a special characteristic to his welcome. Hannah jumps up on you for a body hug; Tina wants to give one soft lick to the tip of your nose; Mary Agnes presents her head for a scratch behind the ears; Mama Sarah rolls onto her back for a stomach rub. The welcome ends only when each one has made his or her particular contribution to the ritual. This much is obvious: you were missed and there is delight all around at your return.

Speaking in terms like obligation and responsibility makes our task seem a chore. It has been my experience that realizing our relationship to creation, and particularly to the creatures, has made awareness of life's beauty, wonder, and joy fuller. Appreciation of my own life and of life in general has been enhanced. Thinking of the regard in which all things are held by their Creator and that all things share in His glory makes the appreciation of all things deeper. Oneness with life and creation gives new dimension to a sense of oneness with God. Everything is more precious; everything is appreciated. Among the kindest, most caring people I have known are those who, feeling a responsibility for creatures and creation, have sought to fulfill it.

There are moments when I sense a wonder about the world in which I live. A sparrow lights in my palm to nibble crumbs. A turtle, being rescued from the middle of the road, doesn't retreat into his shell for fear of me. On the bench a seagull lights on my shoulder to rest and accompany me as I walk along. It is a foretaste of the coming peace and harmony. The wonder and beauty of being alive is unavoidable, as is the feeling that there is indeed something very good about the way God originally created the world. We find a serenity and peace within when we discover harmony with the world about us. Such was the original paradise.

There are organizations and causes committed to the care of creation and creatures with which one might get involved. The extent of that is a personal decision determined by opportunity and personal interests. The essential thing is that we become sensitive to the responsibility and recognize the obligation to all that God has created and given into our keeping.

There are some very simple possibilities. Jesus compared the beginning of the Kingdom of God to a mustard seed, which begins as the smallest of seeds and grows to become a tree in which sparrows nest. There are the "smallest of seeds" we can plant for the creatures. Scattered bread crumbs on frozen ground, hot water on an icy bird bath can be messages of God's love to hungry, thirsty fowl.

An obligation to help injured animals on the roadside and rescue turtles in middle of thoroughfares has seemed a responsibility to me. When traveling alone through the countryside, my personal habit has been to pray for the creatures I see. For fowl, cattle, herds, pets, I have prayed, "Lord, bless them and bring them to your new heaven and earth." For creatures too near busy traffic, I pray, "Lord, protect them." For some I pray that they would know someone's love and for all I give thanks for their practical gifts and/or gifts of beauty to my life and to our world. When I see buzzards at work, I thank God for those who do a job none of us wants. There are grounds for gratitude for every living thing, though I must admit my enthusiasm is weakest for flies, fleas, and cockroaches. But I recognize this as my problem.

More important than the means we find for expression is the realization of our responsibility as God's stewards of His world. Thereby, we undertake our share as God's co-workers in His new creation. Even in ancient Israel, there was recognition of the moral obligation to animals: "A righteous man regardeth the life of his beasts" (Prov. 12:10).

Conclusion

The question with which we began: Is my dog in heaven?
    The biblical answer: Yes, indeed!
    But we have a responsibility!

*   *   *

I have a fantasy: as I enter the gates of heaven, I am greeted by Brownie leading the corps of all the animals I have known. The scene is excited barking, wagging tails, dancing and jumping, each jockeying for a personal touch. It is but a fantasy, but it includes one of my blissful moments from life on earth. Perhaps, the fantasy may not be too far-fetched.